TO:

....
....
....

FROM:

....
....
....

Memories from Mom

my journal of faith and love

Thomas Nelson

Since 1798

NASHVILLE   DALLAS   MEXICO CITY   RIO DE JANEIRO

Published in Nashville, Tennessee, by Thomas Nelson.

Thomas Nelson titles may be purchased in bulk for educational, business, fund-raising, or sales promotional use. For information, please e-mail SpecialMarkets@ThomasNelson.com.

ISBN-13: 978-1-4003-2342-5

Printed in China

14 15 16 17 [LEO] 5 4 3 2 1

www.thomasnelson.com

Contents

Introduction 6

Me and My Family 8

Childhood 12

Teenage Years 52

College Years/New Job Experience 78

Young Adulthood 90

Faith Matters 110

Marriage 134

    Enter: Children 143

The Latter Years 158

Introduction

otherhood is a never-ending job. Days are filled with caring for children and husbands and homes and careers and friends. And oftentimes, amid all the activity and demands, you lose track of the special moments from your past–moments that have shaped you into who you are today.

We invite you to curl up in a comfy chair and start recording some of your best memories in the pages of this journal. Beginning with early childhood and continuing through the different seasons of life, you'll be asked to share details ranging from your favorite food as a child to where you went on your first date. You'll also share about your faith and the role it has played as you've grown and gained from life's experiences. You may have to look up the answers to a few questions, but doing so is a fun way to see changes over the years at a glance.

Recording the memories of your life and faith is time well spent. Doing so will provide your children and grandchildren a chance to know you better—to learn more about who you are as a woman, a mother, a grandmother, and most importantly, a child of God. *Memories from Mom* will be a keepsake for years, even generations, to come.

ME AND MY FAMILY

YOUR Full Given Name

....

The Date of Your Birth

....

The Place of Your Birth

....

Your MOTHER'S Full Name

....

The Date and Place of Her Birth

....

Your FATHER'S Full Name

....

The Date and Place of His Birth

....

The Names of Your Paternal GRANDPARENTS

....

....

The Dates and Places of Their Births

....

....

The Names of Your Maternal GRANDPARENTS

....

....

The Dates and Places of Their Births

....

The Names of Your SIBLINGS

....

....

The Dates and Places of Their Births

....

The Date and Place of Your WEDDING

....

The Full Given Name of Your HUSBAND

....

The Names and Birth Dates of Each of Your CHILDREN

....

....

....

....

A FEW OF MY FAVORITE THINGS

Color ....

Flower ....

Book..

Author ....

Christmas Carol...

Dessert...

Vacation Spot...

Type of Food...

Sport..

Movie ....

Free-Time Activity...

Childhood

WHO WAS PRESIDENT?

....

WHAT BAND WAS MOST POPULAR?

....

HOW MUCH DID A GALLON OF GAS COST?

....

HOW MUCH WAS A LOAF OF BREAD?

....

HOW MUCH WAS A GALLON OF MILK?

....

Who gave you your name...

....

....

and why that name?

....

....

....

....

....

Did you have a **NICKNAME** at home? How did you get it?

....

....

....

....

....

....

....

....

What PETS did you have growing up?

....
....
....
....
....
....
....
....

Which pet was your *favorite?* Why?

....
....
....
....
....
....
....
....
....

HAVING FUN

What was your *favorite* thing to do as a child? Share any details that come to mind on the lines below.

☐ Play with dolls
☐ Play indoor games
☐ Play sports
☐ Ride bikes
☐ Read books
☐ Other

....

....

....

....

....

....

....

....

....

Describe a **PERFECT** summer day from your childhood.

What did your family do on *vacations* when you were growing up? Provide any extra details on the lines below.

- ☐ Go camping
- ☐ Visit relatives
- ☐ Take road trips
- ☐ Stay home
- ☐ Other

Tell of one especially *memorable* vacation experience: when and where you went, who went, and why this particular vacation was your favorite.

....
....
....
....
....
....
....
....
....
....
....
....
....
....
....
....
....
....

There's nothing like a family ROAD TRIP! Describe details from a road trip that you remember most.

....

....

....

....

....

....

....

What did you and your siblings do to pass the time while riding in the car?

....

....

....

....

....

....

....

What words from the front seat did you regularly hear?

....

....

....

....

....

....

....

Describe your first plane ride.

How old were you? Where did you fly and why?

Were you excited? Nervous?

....

....

....

....

....

....

....

....

....

What was your *favorite* meal when you were a kid?

- ☐ mac and cheese
- ☐ fried chicken
- ☐ pot roast
- ☐ pork chops
- ☐ spaghetti
- ☐ hamburgers
- ☐ hot dogs
- ☐ something else:

What **YUCKY FOOD** do you remember your mom making you eat? Do you like it now?

Where did your FATHER go to WORK? What did he do?

....

....

....

....

....

....

....

....

Where did your mother go to work? What did she do?

....

....

....

....

....

....

....

....

....

What did you want to be when you grew up and why? (There can be more than one answer!)

What fear(s) did you experience as a child? What did you do about those fears?

Did you experience any *loss* when you were a child? What did you learn from that experience? How did it shape who you are today?

LEARNING AND RESPONSIBILITIES

What chores did you have to do when you were growing up?

....

....

....

....

....

Which ones did you dislike most?

....

....

....

....

....

....

....

Which chore did you—*be honest!*—not mind doing?

....

....

....

....

Did you get an **ALLOWANCE?**

....

....

....

What did you do to earn that allowance?

....

....

....

....

How much was your allowance—and *what* amount would be
comparable today?

....

....

....

....

Who was your favorite teacher in elementary school? Why?

....

....

....

....

....

....

....

....

....

....

....

....

....

....

....

....

....

....

Did you have a FAVORITE *aunt* or *uncle* or *cousin* or *grandparent* when you were young? What made that person and that relationship special?

....

....

....

....

....

....

....

....

....

....

....

....

....

....

....

....

....

How old were you when you learned to *ride a bike?*

Who taught you? What kind of bike did you have?

Did you *learn* to swim, water ski, or snow ski? To bowl, roller skate, or sail? What do you remember about any of these learning processes?

....

....

....

....

....

....

....

....

....

....

....

....

....

....

....

....

....

....

....

....

Tell about an award, honor, or *special recognition* you received when you were young.

....
....
....
....
....
....
....

What were family finances like when you were growing up, and how did that level of income affect you?

....
....
....
....
....
....
....

What **BEDTIME RITUALS** did your parents regularly do and say before putting you to bed each night?

Describe a typical family BIRTHDAY CELEBRATION when you were a girl.

....

....

....

....

....

....

....

....

What did your family do to make you feel special?

....

....

....

....

....

....

....

....

....

Did you get a BIRTHDAY meal? How many and what kinds of gifts would you receive?

....

....

....

....

....

....

....

Did you play any sports when you were growing up? Did you play a musical instrument?

....

....

....

....

....

....

....

....

....

Think about the house you grew up in. Sketch a floor plan of your bedroom—and, if you want, of the entire house.

....

....

....

....

....

....

....

....

....

What did you see out your *bedroom* window?

....

....

....

....

....

....

....

....

How far away was your SCHOOL, and how did you get there?

....

....

....

....

....

....

What neighborhood friends and activities do you remember?

....

....

....

....

....

....

....

....

....

....

....

....

MAKING MEMORIES

Did you attend family or friend reunions? Share some

MEMORIES from one of your favorite gatherings.

What did your family do to CELEBRATE Easter?

What did your family usually do to celebrate *Thanksgiving?*

And since you can't talk about Thanksgiving without talking about food, what were your favorite items on the Thanksgiving table?

☐ Turkey
☐ Stuffing
☐ Mashed potatoes
☐ Sweet potatoes
☐ Cranberry sauce
☐ Jello salad
☐ Pumpkin pie
☐ Family recipe:

....

....

....

....

☐ Other:

....

....

....

....

Tell about some family *Traditions* that made Christmas special when you were growing up.

Decorating

....
....
....
....
....
....
....
....

Tree

....
....
....
....
....
....
....
....
....
....

Baking

....

....

....

....

....

....

....

....

Wrapping packages

....

....

....

....

....

....

....

....

....

....

Caroling

....
....
....
....
....
....
....

Christmas Eve

....
....
....
....
....
....
....
....
....
....

Christmas morning

....

....

....

....

....

....

....

....

Christmas dinner

....

....

....

....

....

....

....

....

....

REMEMBERING MOM

A FAMILY STORY My Mother Loved to Tell

....
....
....
....
....
....
....
....
....
....
....
....
....
....

A Family Story I Love to Tell *about my mother*

....
....
....
....
....
....
....
....
....
....
....
....
....
....
....
....
....
....
....
....
....

My Mom's Pet sayings and Frequently Stated Words of Wisdom

....

....

....

....

....

....

....

....

....

....

....

....

....

....

....

....

Some of Mom's GOOD ADVICE (you can list more than one piece!)

....

....

....

....

....

....

....

....

....

....

....

....

....

....

....

....

....

....

Teenage Years

WHO WAS PRESIDENT?

....

WHAT BAND WAS MOST POPULAR?

....

HOW MUCH DID A GALLON OF GAS COST?

....

HOW MUCH WAS A LOAF OF BREAD?

....

HOW MUCH WAS A GALLON OF MILK?

....

What were your favorite movies or TV shows during your middle to high school years?

....

....

....

....

....

....

....

Who were your favorite actors and actresses?

....

....

....

Singers and groups?

....

....

....

....

....

What was the name of your **high school?** Its **colors?** Its **mascot?** And—for extra credit—the words of the **alma mater?** (Double extra credit if you can still sing it!)

....
....
....
....
....
....
....
....
....
....
....
....
....
....

What **extracurricular activities** were you involved in during high school? Why did you choose them— or choose not to be involved in any?

Did you have YOUR OWN CAR or drive your parent's car? What color, year, make, and model was the car?

....
....
....
....
....
....
....
....
....
....
....
....
....
....
....
....
....
....
....
....

What did you WORRY about in high school? How did you
handle the things that made you ANXIOUS or afraid?

Did you LOSE anyone close to you or go through any particularly difficult times (or painful times) during this season of your life? HOW did they impact your life?

....

....

....

....

....

....

....

....

....

....

....

....

....

....

....

....

....

....

....

GROWING UP AND OUR CHANGING WORLD

How old were you when you got your *first computer?*

How have today's computers changed since then?

....

....

....

....

....

....

....

....

....

....

....

....

....

How old were you when you got your first *cell phone?*

How have cell phones changed since then?

....

....

....

....

....

....

....

....

....

....

....

....

....

....

....

....

....

....

What—if anything—did you do to celebrate December 31, 1999 (the turn of the century)?

When you were a teenager, what did you *wear?*
What *trends* were popular?

....
....
....
....
....
....
....
....
....
....

And how did you wear your HAIR? How did the guys?

....
....
....
....
....
....
....

Who were your CLOSEST FRIENDS—guys as well as girls?

....

....

....

....

....

....

Describe a typical get-together with friends.
Whose house would you go to? Or did you have a favorite
restaurant where you hung out?

....

....

....

....

....

....

....

....

....

....

What were some of the then-popular figures of speech or slang you and your friends used when you were together?

....

....

....

....

....

....

....

....

....

....

....

....

....

....

....

How old were you when you had your first JOB INTERVIEW?

Who interviewed you? How did it go?

Where did you get your first real paying job? What were your duties? How much did you make an hour? How long did you work there?

....

....

....

....

....

....

....

....

....

....

....

....

....

....

....

....

....

....

....

What were FAMILY FINANCES like when you were in high school? How did the abundance or the shortage of income impact you and your high school years?

Think back to your *first date?* Who was the lucky guy? What did you do? What was your curfew? What made the evening fun? Stressful? Memorable? Did you go out again?

....

....

....

....

....

....

....

....

....

....

....

....

....

....

....

....

....

....

HOORAY FOR WEEKENDS!

What was a FUN Friday night for you and your family? With your high school friends?

What was a *typical weekend* like when you were in high school?

....

....

....

....

....

....

....

....

....

....

....

....

....

....

....

....

....

....

THE OL' ALMA MATER

Did you play any sports? What were they?

....
....
....
....

What SCHOOL CLUBS were you involved in?

....
....
....
....
....

What was your favorite subject?

....
....
....
....

Who was your favorite high school *teacher?*

....

....

....

....

....

What did he/she teach, and what made him/her your favorite?

....

....

....

....

What **VOLUNTEER ACTIVITIES** did you participate in, and why?

....

....

....

....

....

....

Did you go to the **PROM?** If so, what was the *theme* of the dance?

....
....
....
....

Who was your date?

....
....
....

What did he **WEAR?**

....
....

What did your *dress* look like?

....
....
....
....
....

Where did you go for pictures? For dinner? For the dance?

....

....

....

....

Was your prom everything you **EXPECTED** it to be? Why or why not?

....

....

....

....

If you *didn't go* to the prom, why not? What, if anything, did you do instead?

....

....

....

....

....

....

What *year* did you graduate?

....

....

....

How many were in your GRADUATING CLASS?

....

....

....

What did you do with your family to *celebrate?*

....

....

....

What did you do with your friends to celebrate?

....

....

....

....

....

In what ways did you REBEL against your parents or at least push back when they reminded you of family rules, curfews, and school responsibilities?

College Years/
New Job
Experience

WHO WAS PRESIDENT?

....

WHAT BAND WAS MOST POPULAR?

....

HOW MUCH DID A GALLON OF GAS COST?

....

HOW MUCH WAS A LOAF OF BREAD?

....

HOW MUCH WAS A GALLON OF MILK?

....

Did you go to COLLEGE? If so, why did you choose that college or university? If not, what did you do after high school?

....
....
....
....
....
....
....
....
....
....
....
....
....
....
....
....
....

Name of college or university:

....

....

....

....

....

How *far away* from home was it?

....

....

....

....

....

Did you live ON CAMPUS or OFF?

....

....

....

....

....

....

Share a FUNNY ROOMMATE STORY—that may have been annoying rather than amusing at the time.

What is one *life lesson* you learned the first year you
were at college?

....

....

....

....

....

....

....

....

....

....

What did you MAJOR in?

....

....

How many times did you change your *major?*

....

....

....

Who was your **FAVORITE PROFESSOR?**

....

....

....

What did he/she teach, and what made him/her your favorite?

....

....

....

....

Did you *work* while you were going to school?
Describe your job and how much you did or
didn't enjoy it.

....

....

....

What **EXTRACURRICULAR** activities and/
or volunteer work did you get involved in?

....

....

....

....

Where did you meet most of your college/adult friends?

☐ Class
☐ Club
☐ Church
☐ Fraternity/Sorority
☐ Sports
☐ Dorm
☐ Other:

....

....

....

....

Which college/adult *friends* do you stay in touch with?

....

....

....

....

....

....

....

What did you find STRESSFUL about college or your new career? HOW did you deal with the stress?

....

....

....

....

....

....

....

....

....

....

....

....

....

....

....

....

....

....

What were some **DISAPPOINTMENTS** you faced or mistakes you made during your college years or when you were starting your career? What were some lessons you learned?

Young Adulthood

WHO WAS PRESIDENT?

....

WHAT BAND WAS MOST POPULAR?

....

HOW MUCH DID A GALLON OF GAS COST?

....

HOW MUCH WAS A LOAF OF BREAD?

....

HOW MUCH WAS A GALLON OF MILK?

....

FINALLY ON YOUR OWN

When did you first *move out* on your own? Did you have a roommate? Where did you live?

....

....

....

....

....

....

....

....

....

....

....

....

....

....

....

....

What **FIVE ITEMS** (if there were that many) were pretty much always in your refrigerator when you first lived on your own?

- ....
....
....
....

- ....
....
....
....

- ....
....
....
....

- ....
....
....
....

- ....
....
....

Who was the first presidential candidate you VOTED for, and why did you vote for that person? What do you remember about the election, the candidates, the issues, the results?

What were some of the key **WORLD** and **NATIONAL** **EVENTS** the year you turned twenty-one? (Googling your answer to this question is not cheating!)

....

....

....

....

....

....

....

....

....

....

....

....

....

....

....

....

....

What kind of *car* did you drive?

....

....

Did you have a PET? If so, what was it and what was its name?

....

....

What surprised you most about living on your own? What was the most difficult thing?

....

....

....

....

....

....

....

....

....

....

....

....

When did you first realize just how *expensive* life is? Describe the situation that taught you that lesson.

....

....

....

....

....

....

....

....

....

....

....

....

....

....

....

....

....

....

....

What was the first thing you called home for to get *advice?*

What experience(s) taught you that LIFE was more difficult than you thought?

....
....
....
....
....
....
....
....
....
....
....
....
....
....
....
....
....
....

FALLING IN LOVE

When and where did you meet your *husband?*

....

....

....

What first **ATTRACTED** you to him?

....

....

When did you realize you wanted to spend the

rest of your life with him?

....

....

....

....

....

How long did you date before you became engaged?

....

....

....

....

....

....

....

Describe the setting when and where he **PROPOSED.**

....

....

....

....

....

....

....

....

....

....

....

Share some SCENES from your engagement—events or meltdowns, disagreements or happy moments.

....

....

....

....

....

....

....

....

....

How long were you ENGAGED?

....

....

Who, if anyone, did premarital counseling with you?

....

....

....

What **BOOKS** did you read?

....
....
....
....
....
....
....

What *issues* did you wrestle with?

....
....
....
....
....
....
....
....
....
....
....

HERE COMES THE BRIDE!

What were your **WEDDING COLORS?**

....

....

....

What did your *bridesmaids* wear?

....

....

....

What kind of flowers were in your wedding bouquet?

....

....

....

....

What is your wedding/anniversary date?

....

....

....

Where were you MARRIED and who married you?

....

....

....

....

....

What did you serve at the reception?

....

....

....

....

....

....

....

....

....

AND THE HONEYMOON . . .

WHERE did you go?

....

....

....

....

....

....

....

How long did you stay?

....

....

....

....

....

....

....

....

Was there *any moment*—that you can laugh about now—when you wondered, *Who did I marry?*

....

....

....

....

....

....

....

....

What moments do you remember feeling that you were the

HAPPIEST GIRL in the world?

....

....

....

....

....

....

....

....

....

What **CHALLENGES** did you face during the first years of marriage? How did you handle them?

Were there times of heartache or GRIEF during this time in your life? What were your sources of comfort, and what insight did you receive from the experiences?

Faith Matters

Describe when and how you came to *believe in Jesus* as your personal Savior.

Who was especially significant in your SPIRITUAL
JOURNEY? (Think of role models, mentors, teachers,
preachers, even authors.)

Who PRAYED FOR YOU when you were growing up?

Comment on what impact each of the following had on your
spiritual growth during your life.

Parent(s)

....
....
....
....
....
....
....

Friend(s)

....
....
....
....
....
....
....
....

Bible study group

....

....

....

....

....

....

....

....

Pastor/church services

....

....

....

....

....

....

....

....

Sunday school

....

....

....

....

....

....

....

....

....

Youth group

....

....

....

....

....

....

....

....

....

Vacation Bible school

....

....

....

Summer camp

....

....

....

Family devotionals

....

....

....

Daily quiet times

....

....

....

....

....

Prayer

....
....
....
....

Journaling

....
....
....
....

Missions trip(s)

....
....
....
....

Community service

....
....
....
....

What is your first memory of Sunday school?

....
....
....
....
....
....
....
....
....
....
....
....
....
....
....
....
....
....
....

What was the first **BIBLE VERSE** you memorized?

....

....

....

....

....

....

....

What was your favorite *Sunday school song* you remember singing?

....

....

....

....

....

....

....

....

....

What has being a *parent* taught you about God's love for you? Share a couple of those lessons.

Describe your FAMILY TREE OF FAITH. What
Christian legacy, if any, did you inherit?

....

....

....

....

....

....

....

What Christian legacy do you want to leave for
your children?

....

....

....

....

....

....

....

....

Since becoming a Christian, in what ways have you *served God* and His people?

What is your **FAVORITE BIBLE VERSE?** Write out the entire verse below and then tell why and when you chose it.

....
....
....
....
....
....
....
....
....
....
....
....
....
....
....
....
....
....
....

What are two or three Bible verses that have meant a lot to you through the years?

....

....

....

....

....

....

....

....

....

....

....

....

....

....

....

....

What are the ways you have *lived out your faith?*

When has **PRAYER** been richest and most life giving?

When has God's Word truly been a great comfort for you?

....

....

....

....

....

....

....

....

....

What ways of SERVING GOD and His people have been

most challenging? most satisfying?

....

....

....

....

....

....

....

....

....

Describe any experiences with missions you've had. Going, giving, and praying all count.

....

....

....

....

....

....

....

....

....

....

....

....

....

....

....

....

....

Who is your *favorite person*—or people—in the Bible?
Why?

What **STORIES** in the Bible have been among your favorites? Why?

Marriage

WHO WAS PRESIDENT?

....

WHAT BAND WAS MOST POPULAR?

....

HOW MUCH DID A GALLON OF GAS COST?

....

HOW MUCH WAS A LOAF OF BREAD?

....

HOW MUCH WAS A GALLON OF MILK?

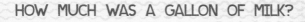

THE FIRST YEAR

Describe the **FIRST HOUSE** or apartment you lived in as husband and wife.

Address:

....

....

....

....

Location:

....

....

....

....

....

....

Share details about the early matrimony *décor*.

....

....

....

....

....

What were some of your standard **MEALS?**

....

....

....

....

What was one *meal disaster?*

....

....

....

....

....

....

Who was usually responsible for these matters of survival?

GROCERY SHOPPING	HIM HER
PAYING THE BILLS	HIM HER
MEAL PLANNING	HIM HER
COOKING	HIM HER
CLEANING	HIM HER
TAKING OUT TRASH	HIM HER
WASHING THE CAR	HIM HER
FILLING THE CAR WITH GAS	HIM HER
MOWING THE LAWN	HIM HER
LOCKING THE DOORS AT NIGHT	HIM HER
FEEDING THE PETS	HIM HER
MAKING THE MORNING COFFEE	HIM HER

Describe from sunup to sundown a typical *weekend*.

What were some of your favorite date nights during your first years of marriage?

☐ Movies at home
☐ Going out to a movie
☐ Dining out
☐ Attending a sporting event
☐ A bike ride
☐ Tennis
☐ The theater/symphony
☐ Going on a picnic
☐ Going to the lake
☐ Other:

....

....

....

....

....

....

....

What are the **FIRST TRIPS** you took together (not including your honeymoon)?

Enter: Children

What was your reaction when you first found out you were *pregnant* (or that your adoption was going through)? You may check more than one box:

☐ Stunned

☐ Ecstatic

☐ Worried about health

☐ Concerned about finances

☐ Filled with joy

☐ Praised God

☐ Relieved

☐ Shock

☐ "Who do I tell?"

☐ "I need to see a doctor!"

☐ Other:

....

....

....

....

How did you tell your parents they were going to be grandparents?

How would you describe each of your **PREGNANCIES?**

Or if you adopted, tell about the adoption process.

What are your *children's names* and why did you choose them?

....
....
....
....
....
....

What aspect of being a **NEW MOMMY** most surprised you?

....
....
....
....
....
....
....
....
....

What was the hardest part of being a mommy during those first three months?

....
....
....
....
....
....
....

And the BEST part?

....
....
....
....
....
....
....
....

What was your *favorite lullaby* to sing? What was your FAVORITE BEDTIME story to read?

Share your best (meaning worst) diaper story.

What did parenting a *newborn* begin to teach you about God's love for you?

....

....

....

....

....

....

....

....

....

....

....

....

....

....

....

....

What did you do to make birthday's **SPECIAL** for your little ones?

....
....
....
....
....
....
....
....
....
....
....
....
....
....
....
....
....
....
....
....

What was/is the hardest part of being a mom of
preschoolers?

....

....

....

....

And the **BEST** part?

....

....

....

....

What did parenting a *preschooler* teach
you about God's love for you?

....

....

....

....

....

What was/is the hardest part of having TEENAGERS?

....
....
....
....
....

And the *best* part?

....
....
....
....
....

What has PARENTING TEENS taught you about God's love for you?

....
....
....
....
....

What did/do you worry about most as a parent?

....

....

....

....

....

....

....

....

....

....

....

....

....

....

....

....

....

What were some of the most DIFFICULT experiences you had after you became a parent?

....

....

....

....

....

....

....

....

....

....

....

....

....

....

....

What **WISDOM** did you gain from going through hard times?

The Latter Years

WHO IS PRESIDENT?

WHAT BAND IS MOST POPULAR?

HOW MUCH DOES A GALLON OF GAS COST?

HOW MUCH IS A LOAF OF BREAD?

HOW MUCH IS A GALLON OF MILK?

PARENTING ADULT CHILDREN

When did your **nest** become **empty?**

What was the **HARDEST PART** of your last baby bird flying off?

....

....

....

....

....

....

....

What was the *best* part?

....

....

....

....

....

....

....

....

....

What is the most challenging aspect of parenting an adult child?

....

....

....

....

....

....

....

....

What has parenting ADULT CHILDREN taught you about God's love for you?

....

....

....

....

....

....

....

....

....

BECOMING A GRANDPARENT

How many *grandchildren* do you have? What are their names and dates of birth?

....

....

....

....

....

....

....

....

....

....

....

....

....

What do your GRANDCHILDREN call YOU?

What is your *favorite* thing about being a grandparent? Your least favorite?

What **SPIRITUAL LESSONS** do you want to leave your grandchildren?

LOOKING AT YESTERDAY . . .

What are some things on your bucket list you've been able to do?

....
....
....
....
....
....
....
....
....
....
....
....
....
....
....

What is your most *embarrassing* moment?

If you could rewind your life, what KEY DECISION would you make differently? Describe the crossroads . . . why you made the decision you did . . . and why you would choose a different path if you had a "do over."

Think about the *tough times* you experienced when you were growing up. Which of those rough situations or seasons were you later able to see how God used for your good? Be specific about the circumstances as well as their value that you later came to appreciate.

Share some specific ANSWERS TO PRAYER that you have experienced over the years.

What are one or two times when God clearly answered

prayers for one of your children?

In what ways has your life turned out DIFFERENTLY than you thought it would when you were younger? How has your faith impacted those differences?

....

....

....

....

....

....

....

....

....

....

....

....

....

....

....

....

....

THINKING ABOUT TOMORROW

If you could go *anywhere* in the *whole world*, where would you go, and why?

....

....

....

....

....

....

....

....

....

....

....

....

....

....

....

What GOALS—personal, professional, spiritual—do you have for yourself for the next five years? The next ten?

What are some things on your bucket list you have yet to do?

What *hopes and dreams* do you have for each of your children?

....

....

....

....

....

....

....

....

....

....

....

....

....

....

....

....

....

....

WORDS TO REMEMBER

What wise words about MARRIAGE do you wish you had heard before you said, "I do" that you'd like to pass on to your children (and grandchildren)?

What advice do you have for dealing with the early days of marriage?

....

....

....

....

....

....

....

....

....

....

....

....

....

....

....

....

What words of *wisdom* about being a parent do you wish you had heard before you became a mom?

Describe how your relationship with JESUS has affected your life—on the day to day as well as on the big picture.

What are some ways you've kept your *relationship* with the *Lord* vibrant and vital over the years that you'd like to impress on your children and grandchildren?

What impact do you hope you have had on the world when your days on earth are done?

Write out how you hope your family will **REMEMBER** you. Put on paper the important things you want to be sure you have said to them. Close with a blessing for your husband, children, and grandchildren.